NOTE TO PARENTS

Welcome to Kingfisher Readers! This program is designed to help young readers build skills, confidence, and a love of reading as they explore their favorite topics.

These tips can help you get more from the experience of reading books together. But remember, the most important thing is to make reading fun!

Tips to Warm Up Before Reading

- Look through the book with your child. Ask them what they notice about the pictures.
- Wonder aloud together. Ask questions and make predictions. What will this book be about? What are some words we could expect to find on these pages?

While Reading

- Take turns or read together until your child takes over.
- Point to the words as you say them.
- When your child gets stuck on a word, ask if the picture could help. Then think about the first letter too.
- Accept and praise your child's contributions.

After Reading

- Look back at the things your child found interesting. Encourage connections to other things you both know.
- Draw pictures or make models to explore these ideas.
- Read the book again soon, to build fluency.

With five distinct levels and a wealth of appealing topics, the Kingfisher Readers series provides children with an exciting way to learn to read about the world around them. Enjoy!

Ellie Costa, M.S. Ed.
Literacy Specialist, Bank Street School for Children, New York

KINGFISHER READERS

level 1

Time

Thea Feldman

KINGFISHER
NEW YORK

KINGFISHER
LONDON & NEW YORK

Copyright © Kingfisher 2014
Published in the United States and Canada by Kingfisher,
175 Fifth Ave., New York, NY 10010
Kingfisher is an imprint of Macmillan Children's Books, London.
All rights reserved.

Distributed in the U.S. by Macmillan,
175 Fifth Ave., New York, NY 10010

Library of Congress Cataloging-in-Publication data
has been applied for.

Series editor: Thea Feldman
Literacy consultant: Ellie Costa, Bank Street School for Children, New York

ISBN: 978-0-7534-7142-5 (HB)
ISBN: 978-0-7534-7143-2 (PB)

Kingfisher books are available for special promotions
and premiums. For details contact: Special Markets
Department, Macmillan, 175 Fifth Ave.,
New York, NY 10010.

For more information, please visit
www.kingfisherbooks.com

Printed in China
9 8 7 6 5 4 3 2 1
1TR/0314/WKT/UG/105MA

Picture credits
The Publisher would like to thank the following for permission to reproduce their
material. Every care has been taken to trace copyright holders. However, if there have
been unintentional omissions or failure to trace copyright holders, we apologize and
will, if informed, endeavor to make corrections in any future edition.

Top = t; Bottom = b; Center = c; Left = l; Right = r

Cover Shutterstock / Samuel Borges Photography, 3 Alamy/Andrew Holt, 4 Shutterstock/
wavebreakmedia, 5 Shutterstock/Adrian Niederhaeuser, 6t Shutterstock/poonsap,
6b Shutterstock/Tatyana Vychegzhanina, 7t Shutterstock/Monkey Business Images,
7b Shutterstock/Bienchen-s, 8–9 Shutterstock/Morgan Lane Photography, 9t Corbis/
Juice Images, 10 Shutterstock/Adrian Niederhaeuser, 11 Shutterstock/oriontrail,
12 Shutterstock/Monkey Business Images, 13t Nutshell Media/Howard Davies, 13b Kingfisher
Artbank/Michael Wicks, 14–15 Shutterstock/Simon Bratt, 16t Shutterstock/Noam Armonn,
16–17 Alamy/Juice Images, 18 Shutterstock/Kotomiti Okuma, 19 Alamy/Purestock,
20 Shutterstock/Simon Bratt, 21 Shutterstock/Adrian Niederhaeuser, 22 Shutterstock/
Richard Paul Kane, 23 Shutterstock/Olga Sapegina, 24 Shutterstock/Yurlick, 25t Shutterstock/
Monkey Business Images, 25b Nutshell Media/Howard Davies, 26 Shutterstock/Ho Yeow Hui,
27 Shutterstock/3445128471, 28–29 Corbis/Ocean, 30–31 Shutterstock/Elena Efimova.

The sun rises.

It is morning.

3

You wake up
in the morning.

Good morning!

What time is it?

The small hand is on seven.

The big hand is on twelve.

It is seven o'clock.

In the morning, you brush your teeth.

You wash your face.

You get dressed.

You eat
breakfast.

Many kids go to school
in the morning.

Many grownups
go to work
in the morning.

The morning ends
at noon.

Both hands of the
clock are on twelve.

At noon, the sun is high in the sky.

Many people eat lunch at noon.

After noon, it is the afternoon!

You get out of school in the afternoon.

After school, you can do
many things.

The afternoon ends
when the sun sets.

Now it is evening.

In the evening,
your family
makes dinner.

Then you get to eat it!

Evening becomes night.

You brush your teeth
and wash your face.

Now you are ready
for a bedtime story!

While you are asleep, the day ends and a new one begins.

This happens at **midnight**.

At midnight, it is very dark outside.

Both hands of the clock are on twelve.

One day is 24 hours long.

One **hour** is 60 minutes long.

A football game
is played for 60 minutes.

One minute is 60 seconds long.

A **second** is as fast as a clap of your hands.

There are seven
days in one **week**.

Monday

Tuesday

Wednesday

Thursday

Friday

Saturday

Sunday

Saturday and Sunday
are also called the **weekend**.

Many people
do not go to
school or work.

There are four weeks in one **month**.

There are 12 months in one **year**.

January	February	March
April	May	June
July	August	September
October	November	December

Everyone has a birthday, once a year, on the day they were born.

When is your birthday?

One year has 365 days.

A new year begins on
January 1.

There are many celebrations
all over the world.

Look!

The sun is in the sky.

It is morning again.

What will you
do today?

Glossary

hour an amount of time that is 60 minutes long

midnight in the middle of the night, when one day ends and another begins. Both hands of the clock are on twelve and it is very dark outside.

month an amount of time that is four weeks long. There are twelve months in one year.

second the time it takes to clap your hands once

week an amount of time that is seven days long

weekend the two days of the week that are also called Saturday and Sunday

year an amount of time that is twelve months long

If you have enjoyed reading
this book, look out for more in
the Kingfisher Readers series!

Collect and read them all!

KINGFISHER READERS: LEVEL 1

Animal Colors ☐
Baby Animals ☐
Busy as a Bee ☐
Butterflies ☐
Colorful Coral Reefs ☐
Jobs People Do ☐
Seasons ☐
Snakes Alive! ☐
Tadpoles and Frogs ☐
Time ☐
Trains ☐
Tyrannosaurus! ☐

KINGFISHER READERS: LEVEL 2

Amazing Animal Senses ☐
Fur and Feathers ☐
In the Rainforest ☐
Sun, Moon, and Stars ☐
Trucks ☐
What Animals Eat ☐
What We Eat ☐
Where Animals Live ☐
Where We Live ☐
Your Body ☐

For a full list of Kingfisher Readers books, plus
guidance for teachers and parents and activities
and fun stuff for kids, go to the Kingfisher Readers
website: **www.kingfisherreaders.com**